Ancient Empty Streets

A Collection of Poems

Ancient Empty Streets

A Collection of Poems

Anirudh R.P.

ZORBA BOOKS

Published by Zorba Books, January 2023
Website: www.zorbabooks.com
Email: info@zorbabooks.com
Author Name : ANIRUDH R.P.
Copyright ©: ANIRUDH R.P.

Title: ANCIENT EMPTY STREETS

Printbook ISBN: 978-93-95217-24-8
Ebook ISBN: 978-93-95217-27-9

Zorba Books Pvt. Ltd. (opc)
Sushant Arcade,
Next to Courtyard Marriot,
Sushant Lok 1, Gurgaon – 122009, India

Printed in India

Contents

Cast Your Dancing Spell on Me

Smoke Rings of My Mind

"Though I know that evening's empire has returned into sand
Vanished from my hand
Left me blindly here to stand, but still not sleeping
My weariness amazes me, I'm branded on my feet
I have no one to meet
And the ancient empty street's too dead for dreaming"

– Mr. Tambourine Man, Bob Dylan

Acknowledgement

If had to begin expressing my gratitude, I'd have to list out names of hundreds of amazing people in my life, who supported, guided, criticized and loved me throughout my life until now. Firstly, I'd love to thank my parents- Mr. P. Ramesh Kumar & Mrs. B.O. Praseeda for being such awesome parents, for supporting me and letting me dream the craziest dreams and helping me achieve it. I'll love you forever. I also thank Kausthubh R.P. and Aiswarya Rajesh for helping me compile my poems and supporting me through thick and thin, as well as for taking the time to do illustrations for this book, which makes it even more beautiful. I'm forever devoted to my grandparents- Mr.A. Balakrishnan Nair & Mrs. Omana Kutty Amma, Mr. P. Prabhakaran Nair and the blessings of Late Mrs. Kasthuri Prabhakaran.

I also express my sincere gratitude to my teachers at school, professors, friends and followers on Instagram for giving me the support and giving me the assurance that its okay to dream big!

Lastly, I thank god for all the opportunities I have in my life, and I'm forever grateful and humbled for that.

Thank you all!

Prologue

It was a cold rainy evening of early 2025, when the car dropped me at home. I could see my Grandparents sitting on the armchairs in the veranda waiting for my arrival. My flight was delayed and I had to go through hell to find a taxi back home on a rainy day like this. 'We were so worried.' My grandmother walked towards me, holding onto my cheeks gently. She was excited to see me after over a year, she pulled me closer to her and kissed on my head. Followed by my maternal grandfather standing up from his arm chair trying to stand steadily and asked me 'How was your journey?' he asked, 'How are your studies?' he added, in his handsome baritone voice. 'Everything is going well Appupa. Right now I'm a little tired.', he nodded exhibiting the army officer discipline that he had always possessed. I turned around to find my paternal grandfather, walking towards me, I gave him the half hug I usually give, he is particularly inexpressive of love but shows it in many other ways leaving his loved ones to comprehend. 'What time did the flight land?' he asked, 'Around 5:30 PM, Appupa.' I said, as I walked into our home.

5 years ago, as an ambitious engineering student, with a patchy beard and a naïve face, I walked into the same home. Back then, I had no emotional connection with it. I've never been at home for more than 2 weeks until then, and little did I know that I would be inside the home for two years following the

dreadful outbreak that I do not wish to recollect. The big and majestic rooms, the expensive interiors and the scenic view from the balcony balcony, my home. Flawlessly crafted to house humans with flaws. The craftsman being my father, the skilled civil engineer with my mother, a hardworking science tutor, as the strongest back bone for all his decisions and aspirations. They definitely are a Power Couple, rising from absolute nothingness without relying on anyone. Inspiring.

Unlike the cold western winds that I'm used to by now, I woke up, the next morning as the heavenly wind gushed into my room through the open windows, the slight chilly air because of the rain from the previous day and the fragrance of nature gave me an energy I've been missing from my life all these years. The sounds of the birds and the cock-a-doodle-doos from the backyard, the moo's and the barks and the sly meows from the neighbor's backyard woke me up.

'Coffee?' My grandmother, had begun the coffee preparations as soon as she saw me walk down into the main hall.

'I'm a Spoilt Kid' I thought. My maternal and paternal grandfathers were reading newspapers and discussing the day's news over tea, with utmost concentration that they didn't notice me walk past them. I stood next to my grandmother, whom I fondly call Ammuma, and looked at her as she switched ON the stove in an attempt to make the coffee. Her trembling hands made it difficult to hold the cup, so I decided to make the coffee myself. Ammuma is a Hindi teacher and a closeted poet, everyone says I inherited my poetry skills from her, well the works genes do are fascinating.

I grabbed my cup of coffee and slowly walked back into the hall, when I saw a small book stand that was placed unusually in the stair case room. Usually the book stand was kept at the library in the first floor. I walked towards the dusty book stand. It was a small plastic book stand that wasn't aesthetically pleasing. Dusty hard bound books, worn out diaries labelled 1997, 2001, 2004 and 2013, the pages were damaged and the ends were thumbed in most of the books. Beneath them all, I found a file. Ironically, the file looked as if the entire stand was made to preserve that one precious file. The white shiny bind, still remained shiny. The hundred pages still looks fresh after all these years, I flipped the file wiping out the little dust and the cobwebs at the ends and looked at the front page, 'My Poems', the title read, and a small photograph of the legendary song writer Bob Dylan was stuck below the title. There was an amateur front cover design too, with my name neatly written.

'2020', I thought, that's where it all began. The solitude that made me embark on a mission to showcase my emotions in the best way possible. A way to make everyone realize, they are not alone and to lend a helping hand. The solitude that changed my life, the solitude that opened a new path that remained undiscovered by me till them, a path that remained hidden within me, a path that I can't forget. The Ancient Empty Streets

The Ways of the World

There was a time when I was drowned
in an endless stream of dilemma and pain,
Anxiously waving my arms, in an attempt
To Aimlessly swim against the tides,
Clueless, still holding onto a pride.
When the stream began flowing stronger,
Pushing me farther away,
The world looked at me in pity that day.
But there was just one man, who swam
Risking his life, to save mine.
Against the rising tides for me,
One day, I would remember his name.

When the whole world around me felt like collapsing.
When the safe shelter over my head began falling.
When there was no one who would answer me
wailing, and crying for help,
when everyone walked past and
when some of them walked over me.
Then came the man, who stepped in
and held me tight and said-
Son, you ain't a weakling as they say.

And then he waved goodbye
As he showed me the right way.
And promised to reappear someday.

Years later, when I grew a little mane,
I grew up to look just the same-
As the man who saved me from
Every other pain,
I stood beside him today, taking pride.
The little quarrels disappear,
In minutes, then he reappears,
And I look into his eyes when he says-
Son, life is like a little bus,
You wait till it arrives,
But once you get in don't forget,
For the destination, you wish for,
Is a really long drive,
The patience you possess is
the key to your surviving,
The rough ways of this world.

He was my father,
Who taught me the ways of the world,
The good, bad and ugly faces of life,
He was the man who taught me the
secrets ways of the world,
and told me, one day,
it would pave my path.

The Little Father

Back when I was around 3 ft. tall,

I saw my parents hold a tiny boy in their arms,

They said he looked like me,

They taught him to call me his brother.

I was a restless and fidgety boy,

I wasn't so responsible as a child either,

But, When the tiny innocent arm, held onto my thumb.

I knew, I had to change into someone better,

When I spotted a magical innocence in his smile,

I knew, I had to become better for him.

Everyone called him the baby of our house,

Often times, he'd look around with his big round eyes,

In an attempt to unlock the mysteries

of the world around him, as he sees.

I held him in my arms, one evening,

And kissed him on his cheeks, not once, but many times,

And then laid him on my shoulder slowly,

As I walked around, patting his back gently.

My young tender palm caressing his tender head,

as his face comfortably laid on my shoulder.

He was fast asleep, on his brother's shoulder.
On my shoulder, and I smiled.
I sense of pride, and accomplishment swept,
I silently laid him on the bed,
And placed a pillow beside him.

Our parents looked at us happily,
A little father, they said, with pride.
I shyly looked at the baby,
Well he did look like me,
As I gently turned around,
Smiling while he was asleep.

When I was well over 5 ft. tall,
I was far away from the little me,
He grew up to be smarter,
And a better version of me.
From a distance, I looked at him,
'My brother' I'd whisper, with pride.
From a distance, I looked at him,
'That's me.' I'd whisper, with pride.

Mother - A Poem Herself

When my father carved the world around me,
Introducing challenges to motivate me,
When he watched me fall and rise,
With pride filling up as tears in his eyes,
There was someone who nurtured me,
Sowed the seed within, and nurturing-
With an innate innocence and focus,
Bring me up to be the best version,
The wonderful passion that she exhibits,
Towards everything she does.
The childlike innocence,
The intense hardwork and sacrifice,
The affection in her eyes and touch.
Me being the flower she nurtured,
In her beautiful orchard,
Grew up to be colorful,
And so
were the other flowers she nurtured.
Every flower calls her by different names,
Some call her 'the teacher',
While I call her Mother,
Mother, the most fascinating poem herself.

The Beautiful Dawn of Twenty-Twenty

There was a silence too incomprehensible,
The dim ray of sunlight, through the dark clouds,
The beginning of a new day, a dawn of hope,
A passage to pursuing everything you could.
Yet, I was imprisoned,
stripped off the virtues of life.
Yet, I was imprisoned,
and so was everyone around me.
An empty balcony after a rainy night,
Welcoming the glorious day light.
With me holding onto the parapet,
Looking at the dense trees behind my home.
The sounds of the birds chirping,
The sounds of car zooming through the roads,
The empty streets, which felt stranded.
While I looked at the sky, for a sign.
An old earphone plugged into my ears,
An old tambourine man playing songs
For me, and me alone.

An old tambourine man, putting me to sleep,

In an attempt to wake a new me,

An old tambourine man, enlightening me,

The beginning of a new day.

The Shadows I Chase

POrtraying EMotionS

Freed, One Day

A noise up in my head clouded the vision
The path less taken, with thorns yet its passion.
Like soulless music, I yelled at my fate.
For my misery to end, how long should I wait?

I smile at the world, choosing to be happy,
Until my face turns stiff and the world turns snappy.
I smile at the world, choosing disappointment,
Until I turn stiff, losing hope and attainment.

A day would come, and as the sun rises.
When the world is freed from all its crisis.
When life turns ordinary, those million dreams.
When I could walk a free man, marching to my dreams.

A day would come, a day not so far.
When I forget to cover my face
When we live in peace, over caste and race
When the mask still lays unused, misplaced.

I wish for a day when I could meet my friends
Talking to them, like there is no end,
And still not worry that the world, that'd betray
And still not worry that you'd go astray.

I wish for a day when I meet my loved ones.
Hug them gently and tell them tales of bygones.
Hoping that the world forgets and forgives,
And bring back the happier days to relive.

The Wild Tranquility

Trailing the path taken thousands of times
Echoes of a holistic chant, a loud bell that chimes.
Ringing in unison, sharp sounds that could calm
Volcanoes that are no longer dormant, without harm.
A hundred emotions rekindled like a fire burning bright,
Like the sound of that one dried lead that falls off the branches
Slowly making its way to a clean stone courtyard.
Like the hand-carved inscriptions on the rock walls
And the patience they teach us, it all falls.
Walking through the silent corridor of the monastery,
Seeking a wild moment of tranquility.
Fingers following the deep carvings in the wall
The stories of the men who lived, without saying it all.
Like the moment when the evil within sleep for good,
When the animosities and vengeance are lost in time.
When the pain and pleasure are words that rhyme.
Like the moment that tiny heat escapes from your soul
Without you trying to let it out, all the more.
The enchanting sounds of the brooms on the ancient floors

The sounds of the chirping birds, like the folklores.

Trailing the path taken thousands of times

Never to return to those awful times.

I won't escape, I'd face it with integrity,

But only after seeking a wild moment of tranquility.

Deranged

I had plans, gazillions of them, like the stars in the sky
But, like guests uninvited invading our path,
The stiff smile, the pain, the pleasure, and the wrath,
Standing alone and steady on the cornerstone, deranged.
I silently watched the man in me, change.

I had a principle, one that doesn't let me drown,
In the deep blue ocean of thoughts, a swirl that makes me
frown.
I held onto that one cornerstone, standing rugged;
like a symbol of hope, worthy as a gold nugget.
Standing alone and clumsily holding the cornerstone,
deranged.
I silently watched the man in me, change.

I had one thought, the blazing light at the end of the tunnel,
but the story of my life, a dreamy yet vicious cycle in hell.
I couldn't hold onto that cornerstone, it faded, farther away.
The hopes were shattered, that one miserable day.
But, I seek for that one cornerstone, on the high ranges-
While watching what happens, when the man in me
changes.

Irate

The comforts of my brown armchair began to fade,
the consequences of the hopeless mistakes I've made.
The dents on the walls of my dingy room have stories
to tell.
Ten thousand thoughts upon which I could dwell.
A scream without passion, an overpowering parasite;
Like the mind of a tyrant, as tyrannous was he-
from the colossal ruins, as it's meant to be.
What have I become, what has this led me to?
A voice unknown that pierces through-
The one that I detest, the one that I fear.
Oh, the one that I no more wish to hear.
The comforts of my brown armchair began to fade,
the consequences of the hopeless mistakes I've made.
The bruises on my knuckles have stories to tell-
The stories, are like a wicked wizard's spell.
The ones I'd wish to forget, but the scars do swell.
I'm drenched even on a cold winter night-
I couldn't catch my breath all right.
What have I become, what has this led me to?
The bleeding never stopped, nor did the anger-
The one that I would want to let out-

But the one that wouldn't sort out.

The comforts of my brown armchair began to fade,

the consequences of the hopeless mistakes I've made.

The broken possessions of my room, have stories to tell.

The days that I'd walk into the welcoming doors of hell.

The days I'd wish to overcome, until my memory chimes
that bell.

It's traumatizing and stripped me of hope.

Inadvertent chaos, being choked by a thin rope.

What have I become. what has this led me to?

I've screamed silently a million times, and out loud once.

But the story never came to an end, though I seek for one-

Or I'd be stuck in a vicious cycle of pique, one or none.

The Thin Line

Oh! fading lines of time, all the smoke screens appearing

Like an old freezing man on a warm summer evening.

What is true and what isn't, it's hard for me to judge.

Every mistake I've made, and on me, I'd hold my grudge.

Every waking hour, I feel like a tornado-struck theme park.

Every night I sleep, haunted by the thoughts, painfully dark.

Can I be what I wanna be? Am I doing everything right?

I hear a voice in my head, a lot like mine. and its not alright.

Why do I feel like there is a war in my head?

Where the chaos just broke out, and everyone's dead.

When was the last time, I laughed like a baby?

Few days, No Months, I guess a Few Years maybe!

What is that one thing that sucked the life outta me?

Was it hope or the dream or the will to be free.

I'm blindfolded, handcuffed, and bleeding, can you see?

And thrown and left to drown in the big blue sea.

But, what is true and what isn't, it's hard for me to judge.

Every mistake I've made, and on me, I'd hold my grudge

When I got Nothing, I got Nothing to Lose

I stand frozen amidst the heat waves,
A summer afternoon on my balcony.
A hundred different decisions that I took, and
Ambiguities, every worm that fell off the hook.

The hot steam from the coffee cup rising above,
I carried the entire thought in my head right now.
Oh! Nothing feels beautiful at this stage.
Even the things that I loved. Am I in a cage?

I go around smiling, There's nothing to refuse.
When I've got nothing, there is nothing to lose.
The strings of my life are now let loose.
Countless hours alone, my silent peruse.

I walk like an aimless man through the street,
Pulling a colossal rope, until the ends meet.
Falling a hundred times, standing straight once.
Oh! This has been happening for months and months.

The stairs to the top are broken, so you better watch your steps.
One mistake you'll fall to the bottom, oh! those major mishaps.
I ain't living a cowardly life to walk back from you.
I take a deep breath and maybe take a step or two.

I'm as invisible as any man, in a big world I diffuse,
When I've got nothing, there is nothing to lose.
The strings of my life are not let loose.
Countless hours alone, my silent peruse.

Twisted Sorrow

Don't look back, it's all right, it's one crazy shadow.

Driving you through dark rivers, that isn't shallow

It isn't me hiding from those shadows I followed,

Farther from my crazy reign of a twisted sorrow.

Once you walk across the path, my friend, never turn around-

Never turn around to see the road, never sulk or frown.

The reasons behind every choice you take sings

The words in your head back then, thoughts and things.

We never understood the way of life, diabolical or calm

Jumping off the cot every day, swiping off an alarm.

Questioning all the choices we've been making,

And then the silly qualms about literally nothing.

Ain't those the clowns you failed to recognize,

Those that laugh at you behind your back, realize!

Aren't you amused when the car drives past the puddle,

Or are you grumpy and soulless, amidst all the hustle?

You go around sulking about your life, you got no hold.

Mining like a machine for that tiny hidden gold,

Still, you run around, oh you can't let lose,

That screams the silent offers that you can't refuse.

But. Don't look back, it's all right, it's one crazy shadow.
Driving you through dark rivers, that isn't shallow
It isn't me hiding from those shadows I followed,
Farther from my crazy reign of a twisted sorrow.

The Timeless Ballad

Time rolling like a tumbleweed in the Albuquerque outskirt,

Aimlessly swept by the winds, foothills, or back to the dirt,

Or, like sand through the fingers, can't contain them forever.

Or, like a snail that drags itself while anticipating your lover!

Beyond the conspirators, the ones Caeser couldn't see through,

It unveiled itself, with time, with vigor and grandiose it grew.

The mighty one couldn't comprehend, all friends he said-

Until his soul startled and laid there dead in bloodshed!

Time and Trust weren't constants they learned-

With bloodshed and pain, the tables have turned!

Times, they're changing, even before us knowing

Times, they're changing, when we're all-seeing.

I don't deserve the praise or your worthy adoration.
Rather put me behind the bars of life, beyond salvation!
But rip me not, of my comprehension and eyes.
To look at the whole world, beyond your lies.

The world around me disappeared in the evil rings of time,
Like the actors walking off their stage, to a mysterious chime.
The lights turn off, and the curtains close to darkness,
But the story remains, told and retold, the unlooked agelessness.

Time and Trust weren't constants they learned-
With bloodshed and pain, the tables have turned!
Times, they're changing, even before us knowing
Times, they're changing, when we're all seeing.

Dilemma of Life

Millions of ways to write your own story,
Hundreds of crossroads sounds a bit scary-
But you live through it, and you'd decide
The story of your life ain't a thing to hide.

The choices you make may be a colossal mistake-
Or like a million-dollar lottery that you never take.
Sometimes, it's like a little simpleton, never to bother-
Sitting at the corner of the street, in chaos altogether.

This way or that, the strange dilemma of the arctic terns-
Flying by the winds, across those huge groups of ferns.
Or the land where the sands storm their way around
Where the sun never sets, no water is found.

The little bird went in search of the ferns and the
flakes-
And the icebergs, the cold winds, and the frozen lakes.
But then the sands that storm looked great in the middle,
The artic tern switched paths but died a cripple.

Would the ferns have welcomed with their arms open-?
Should we sigh, and move on, it had to happen.
Could it have been any different, a longer life ahead?
Or was that the end of the story- all alone and dead.

Millions of ways to write your own story,
Hundreds of crossroads sounds a bit scary-
But you live through it, and you'd decide
The story of your life ain't a thing to hide.

The Lifeless Nights

Startling thoughts strike at the middle of the night,

When the wind stops gushing through the windows on the right.

A silent yet desperate need to restart your life all over again,

The little discomfort of straying away from that golden lane.

You think about the irreparable mistakes you've made,

While forgetting all the good moments, you've just made them all fade-

away, down the road to the oceans, vanishing by the horizon.

But you just ain't happy with yourself and there ain't any reason.

The rings of aimless smoke ruthlessly blind the road to be taken,

Beds of roses never made sense, bleeding because of the thorns, aching.

I look back at the ruins from time to time, hazy eyed and hurt,

Refusing to toil tirelessly, to rebuild a castle from the dirt.

I don't suffer secretly in silence; nor do I cry out loud-
I have the plans but still, I hide beneath a dark shroud
Toil till the dawn just brings a smile onto your face-
Voila, my friend, you're back in the race.

Startling epiphanies strike in the middle of the night,
The wise ones decide to follow them right.
A silent yet desperate need to pave your life well,
Finding salvation, heaven through hell.

A World too Big

There were forests and lakes, town squares and the
fountains,
Then came the barren lands, soon after those towering
mountains.
Yet the train was on track and the rhythms that followed,
Life lessons, I thought, a pill too hard to swallow.

The love for my life and the world has disappeared,
I shut myself inside a box never to reappear.
My long beard turned grey, and my hair shabby.
Unable to recover, unable to be happy.

I grew weary and selfish; I never bothered to care.
My wrath grew beyond control, still being unaware.
The four walls grew larger as my mind shrank-
Unable to comprehend the world, all plain blank.

I found mistakes in the greens of the nature,
The grey skies appeared too bright.
The gushing wind felt irritable,
yet the dim sunlight seemed tolerable.

The world was too big for a small man like me,

A mystery too complex, too complex to see-

The little things that matter made more sense,

Than the colossal ruins of the life that dubbed nonsense.

Poorly Made

He ran through the paths less chosen,
Yet he was dissatisfied.
He ran through the crowds, blindfolded,
He was petrified.

He ran past the rains and the storms on the way,
Forgetting himself eventually just living each day.
He swam against the deadly tides,
To build his empire, his crazy ride.
His wealth grew beyond borders so fast,
But every morning striked him with mighty aghast.

He made the most beautiful things,
Yet he was poorly made, who'd think?
He forgot who he was over time,
He life has turned into a cacophony in a beautiful chime.
He lived a life, unforgettable for others,
Yet so forgetful for himself.
Everyone who knew him, thought they know him too well.,
Yet he didn't know himself.

His passion has died,

To himself he's lied.

That life was all about this, running a race until he's gone.

He turned out miserable, very soon he'd be all alone.

He made the most beautiful things,

Yet he was poorly made, who'd think?

His empire expanded far and wide,

But now, nobody stood by his side.

Beyond the walls

You can't take those small talks,
Or the never ending rants over a walk,
With the men and the women in your streets,
That you aren't going to explore.

A sense of fear, when someone's near-
Would you want to run away from here?
The calls remain unanswered,
The texts remain unread.

You may still be alive,
But you wish you were dead.
Thriving for the undisturbed calmness of the nights,
Fearing any conversation in the broad daylight.

Although you mind your own business,
But you won't be able to witness;
The big world beyond the walls you've built.
Beyond the walls, until it falls.

You stutter and panic on the sidewalks, on your toe-
As you stroll back home, the only world you know.
You break a sweat first, and now you're all drenched.
These are the reasons you get your heart wrenched.

You can't take the complexity of the world around you,
The world and your life is beyond your comprehension.
Hence you bid adieu to the world so wide & expanding-
Stuck here unable to move, so disappointing.

Although you mind your own business,
But you won't be able to witness,
The big world beyond the walls you've built.
Beyond the walls, until it falls.

Abyss to Abyss

I don't fear the inevitable.

I don't fear the past.

A life so diabolical and despicable,

Yet how long does it last

I remained off the radar for years,

I tried to forget myself, holding back my tears.

The identities I created to cope with my emotions,

How cowardly of me to run away from the human commotions.

I've seen the darkness,

I've seen the light.

Though, I tried to witness it all,

With all my might.

I remained broken often times.

Chasing an inexplicable void.

Is living this life a crime?

Then it's a crime I can't avoid.

But, why bother if life is about being born crying- and die being cried for?

A journey from the abyss to the abyss,

A travel from nothingness to nothingness.

But, why bother if life is all about leaving behind

your pain, struggle and legacy,

Or maybe being a timeless hero in some media fantasy.

Or maybe a nobody, never to exist.

With time. I learn to be fearless of the inevitable,

Accepting the past as much as possible.

A life so diabolical and despicable-

And a life as a man so unamicable.

Forgetting Myself

A thought has been blinding
my sight & fogging my brain
in inexplicable ways.
A thought that could rip me of
the love that I wish I had for myself.
A thought so ruthless, that I wish
I was dead the moment I began thinking
About it.
A thought that brought in front of my eyes,
The moments of grief and the doubts on myself,
The things that I couldn't do,
The things that I lacked.
The things that I wish I had never done,
And the things that I wished I possessed.
Forgetting my true self,
my true identity,
I wander seeking a home in a
Home that's not mine.
I wander aimlessly, doing things,
That I'm not good at,
And eventually fail, and the cycle continues.
There is no end, it's a vicious cycle,

Once I stepped in, there seemed to be no return.

Yet, I hope for the light shining bright,

At the end of the tunnel.

I hope for the light shining so bright,

One day, when all the struggles with myself ends.

The Inexplicable Solitude

I'm not afraid of being lonely,
But that has not been the case always.
There were times when I spend a day-
Laughing with people,
I believed would be with me
Forever
I shared every detail of my life
Loved them dearly,
Cared for them.
Guided them throughout
and spoke to them when they were low
and spoke for them fearlessly.
Then they vanish,
They find happiness in a place
somewhere else.
Somewhere beyond me,
Beyond my affection.
Someplace beautiful but unknown to me.
They found solace in a place beyond me.
Yet their laughter reverberates,
in my heart,
A sound that's fading as it moves farther

On a road not far away.
I don't leave traces of affection,
Nor require any attention.
I have no one to meet,
there's not a soul
I wish to waste my smiles on.
I don't smile, I lost the innocence
I was once known for.
I don't smile, I'm alone.
And that loneliness is what I yearn for.

Hope?

Oftentimes. I won't realize,

The bright day turns into nothing but darkness,

And my world is illuminated by the light,

From the screen of my drained laptop,

The empty pens, and the filled spiral books,

And a thousand files, I'd navigate through.

Yet, I don't sense hope, even if there's one.

I don't sense hope, by now, I know there's none.

I try to manifest and then work all day,

digging at the same spot,

in an attempt to carve a long way.

I don't know what needs to be done,

To make things right,

I give up on everything I've ever dreamt of,

Embracing my solitude,

Embracing it all.

The silence of the night, kindles the emotions locked in,

The warmth of the dawn rekindles the optimism,

But The hustle and bustle of the day in between,

Questions everything I've ever built, my dream.

Yet, I surf through the books, look out at the world,

For the tireless toil of the common men and women to inspire me,

Yet. I don't sense hope, even if there's one.

I don't sense hope, by now, I know there's none.

The Silence of the Nights

I'm afraid of the night,
Not because of the darkness,
Not because of the eerie silence,
Not because of the nightmares
That might appear in the middle.
Not because of the fear of beginning
a new day just to suffer again,
Not because I'll have to survive another day,
Carrying a childish smile to hide my pain.
But the thoughts,
The thoughts at night petrify me.
The screaming pessimism,
A silent voice in my head.
The nights that destroyed me,
That ruined me inside out.
Now, only the ruins remain,
The violent breeze has died out.
The violent breeze has died.
Now the thoughts have faded,
Yet the fear remains,
The fear remains.

A Girl Named Hope

When I looked around
the world wasn't the same,
The people I knew long time back,
Looked and sounded different.
I was stuck in a maze not so long ago,
A place ruled by chaos,
I took all the paths, hastily, although
The path to be taken, nobody knows.
But. I wasn't alone,

I had a companion in the journey,
Through the darkness of the path,
With the light from her heart.
She didn't know my name,
Nor did I know hers.
But. I called her Hope.
Yet we stayed true to each other,
Like the last people on the earth,
As the strange mysteries of the maze,
we unearth

I wasn't alone,
I had a companion in the journey,
Through the dead ends,
Through the dangers,
Through the chain of failures,
Until we reached the end,
The free world.
I had her holding my hands tightly,
As we ran out of the maze.
I bid her goodbye, she faded into thin air.

But then I realized,
I'm stuck in a maze called life now,
A place ruled by endless chaos,
The paths were unknown,
The path to be taken, nobody knows,
But now, I didn't have hope,
I was all alone.

Through the Window

When I sit in the solitude of my dim lit room,

A comfortable space, a place that's only mine.

The four walls that have witnessed

the various emotions. I've emoted.

That one warm light in the corner,

A light so dim, yet manages to light up my room,

Feeding into melancholy.

and the thoughts that thrive on melancholy.

An Einaudi orchestral piece

playing gently through the speakers,

Pouring rain, and the gentle breeze

through the opened windows.

I sit up, legs crossed, looking out-

Through the window.

I hope for me in the future

Climbing into my room, through the opened windows.

And guide me through the right path.

But, no one appeared.

And my fear of failure doesn't seem to disappear.

Through the window,

I look out at the whole world,

Convincing myself of the billion opportunities,

Either let thousand men and women live by your shadow,
Or you live in the shadow of other opportunistic men and
women.
There are no more options, just these.
Just two herds in the world.
Two herds aimlessly ran towards the void.
Still, the melancholy persists in the world,
Listening intently and helplessly at
the silent screaming of everyone in solitude.

These Little Moments

Standing alongside the raging tides,

The gentle breeze from the oceans,

And all the worries you leave beside.

The feet struggling as you walk

through the soft therapeutic sand.

barefoot, feeling the earth in its purest form.

The breeze that messes your neatly combed hair,

But ironically every mess in your life,

Feels cleaned up.

It's like falling in love for the first time,

An inexplicable excitement,

A feeling of rejuvenation over remorse,

Teleportation at the finest, taking you to another world.

The beige shorts, and an oversized white shirt,

With a beach ball, and your feet molded in the dirt.

These little moments that matter.

When the professionals fling 30 pages of hard work,

Onto your face, leaving you flustered with anger.

As you walk through the crowded streets of the suburb.

On a dull day, when the clouds turn grey,

On the verge of slight soothing rain,

You find a tiny stall and the aroma of tea drags you,

When you hold it by the brim, the hot tea,

may it be a lemon mint tea or the traditional chai,

and sip it slowly, looking at the world as a new person

An inexplicable excitement.

A feeling of rejuvenation over remorse,

One solution to all the problems,

One solution to the problems of today.

Be here now, the moment that's here.

Be here now, and not in tomorrow's fear.

Because there would be a time much later,

When you realize, that these little moments are

what matter.

Stranded

In the end, no one's gonna stick around,
Even when you're helpless and stranded,
dumbfounded.
Walking miles, covered in dust and dirt,
Make you question everyone's worth.
Some manage to suck your blood,
Some manage to suck your soul,
Leaving you alone, until you're dead,
Leaving you alone as a whole.
I ain't gonna trust anyone again,
All my efforts end up vain.
Let me get off the ride, when I'm sane.
Let me get off before I suffer the pain.
You got your hands holding you tight,
Nobody holds it for you,
You won't have to worry about fights,
You won't have to worry
Because it's you.
Some manage to feed on your brain,
Some manage to turn you insane.
Leaving you alone, until you're dead,
Leaving you forever stained.

Lock Away

You aren't the same person that you used to be,
You wish for life alone.
You don't talk much now,
Though you were known to be a raconteur.

You were known, for your voice, and a charm so undying
But you chose to change,
You forced a change,
Seeking shelter from the storms,
Seeking shelter, following all the norms,
Seeking shelter, as someone you're never supposed to be.
Seeking shelter, and locking yourself away forever.

You were around men and women,
whom you kept happy with the stories you tell,
Now, the same people dread you, afraid that you might yell-
The smiles that you created,
The memories you've made,
And the successes derived
From The hurdles in your path,
Have now vanished,
The consequences of your wrath.

You look at your own plate in a restaurant so crowded,
The clinking sounds of the cutlery and you vibe so well
now.
The huge screen in the cinemas, and your favorite movie-
The whistles and cheers, and the crowd around you, have
reduced to
soft claps slowly.

The invitation chats to the various parties remain
unopened
And so have the WhatsApp groups
created by your friends for tours
No, This ain't maturity.

This is cowardice.
Cowardice to face reality,
Cowardice to face the truth.
Yet, one day when you step out,

You may be the same person from the past,
Your magnetic smile, and the charming voice
would still make people happy.
Because the person from the past never fades away, but
suppressed.
But one day they would show up, the real you
decompressed.

Day Again

Through the tinted windows, a dim ray of the morning
sun crept in

I woke up, sluggishly, like every other day:

like, every other day.

The days felt the same, it may be a game that I'm not
aware of.

The days could be dubbed lame, or am I trailing off my
starlit aim

I manage to spend the time, spending the time without
hope but fear.

The fear that this day would end without a meaning

The fear that this day would start over,

with the sun gleaming.

Invisible drops of sweat pave their way down my forehead,

the scars they etch, oh, where has it led?

The dim moonlight and the silence among the stars

gives me hope of a day, not so far.

When I could express the flavors of a day,

diverse than ever, what more could I say.

The Magic Swirling Ship

Ballads & Tales

The Funny Common Man

The infamous vanishing of the common man,

behind a thing, made his voice as loud as it can.

The Million spectators are the suspects, where they stand.

Bring down the ruins of that man, they don't understand.

The man reappears once he walks off the stage,

like a bird just flying out, upon opening a cage.

The man who walked into the main hall with a smile,

Buries his face in his palm, in tears as he walks a mile.

The common man who made people laugh out loud,

Walks alone on a winter night, hidden beneath a shroud-

And what makes him the man we knew, some time back,

in a fancy suit and funny voice, he knows what we lack

Now, there was a different man walking into someplace shady-

Tears soaking his collar, a sight for which we weren't ready.

Listen good, this is the story of that funny man, who vanishes-

behind a thing, that made his voice as loud as it can.

The Ballad of a Travelling Man

The rhythms of the tracks brought a thought to my head,
The empty bogies, the striking wind, but tired eyes instead
I stumbled upon a traveling man walking across the aisle-
Who looked around and sat in front of me. with a smile.
His beard was grey, it was long and it flowed down-
The wrinkles on his face told a story of his own.
The shabby attire and a shining guitar, intriguing as it was-
And the traveling man, and his journeys across.
The writers and poets around whom I spent my life
and mind-
Taught me nothing but to be selfish and unkind.
The little traveling man never spoke a word yet-
I learned a lot, and I felt, to him, I was in debt.
When you showed me a new path that I've never walked-
A path of patience and innocence, and the doors I've never
knocked on.
The feeling unexpressed and the hundred ballads remain
unsung,
Yet the little traveling man seeks one.
Times when the words on paper never made sense,
A journey within a journey, that's quite intense.

Instead, I should just sing the songs that remain unsung,
Yet the little traveling man seeks one.
When the passions and expressions are too wide to say.
But you'll win them all one by one, someday.
Till then, live your life like the little traveling man-
Oh, keep your eyes open every moment, when you can.

Farewell Ballad

Two men on horseback,
Galloping along the same route.
On the same pace, the same path,
Both of them desired to halt
At the same glorious destination.

One of them knew the art
of judging the time
by the position of the sun,
the other had the entire
path etched in his memory.

They galloped, together, as companions
For hours and days altogether,
They never stopped at first,
Then, They'd stop to quench their thirst,
Then, they'd stop for hours
unable to move,
but. the flashes of the
glorious destination,
never lets them stray away.

Days later, the apprehensive riders,
Reached the crossroads in the path.
One with the art of judging time,
Chose the one that's faster.
The one with the memory of the path,
Chose the harder one.

It was hard to bid farewell.
But the inevitable has come.
The men, never met again, as they bid adieu
and slowly galloped away from each other,
Two men on horseback,
The Musketeers' they say.
Galloping along the same path,
Now never to see each other,
They wave goodbye,
Until they meet again,
at the glorious destination.
But. it won't be the same,
Only the fond memories remain.

A Man from Eastern Ville

There was a mysterious tale in the eastern ville,
About a man, who appears at times to kill-
the fugitives and criminals hiding from the law,
taken down by a fugitive trusted by the law,
and disappears until it's time.

They say he was taller than anyone,
They claimed his strength was unimaginable,
They say his baritone voice
would send shivers down the spine.

They say that all the women in the ville,
Would claim - 'He's mine!'.
No one knew when he would appear,
When he does, it ain't any celebration.
The sharks and petty thieves were petrified,
Until they are lifeless and cold,
and he disappears.
No one knew his name,
A thick black handkerchief,
covering his face.

The only man to be feared by a police chief,
In his glorious hay days.
They say they've heard stories of him,
Pulling triggers as he punishes the-
Weak criminals of the eastern ville.

Yet, no one knows the truth behind it.
Today, the mysterious man is weak and old,
The man who sent shivers down the spine,
Couldn't stand straight without moaning in pain.
The man, who was feared by the fugitives from the law,
Fears the inevitable death.
No one knows his name even now,

But, even hay days have an end,
And so do the bad days.
Time is just a rolling stone,
Rolling down a mountain, uncontrollably.
As it crashes down to the earth, nothing would remain.
Like the last breath of the mysterious man,
His final disappearance.

The Battle Within

He couldn't see the island,
The strong one-eyed man.
Looking into a distance,
Stressing his eye,
His precious eye.
His wide smile hid itself,
behind the overgrown beard,
black and dense,
yet his face, so intense.
Two Hundred ships sank
before his eyes,
Two Thousand men
Burnt alive,
Yet his one-little eye shone bright
Laying out the plans alright.
With the enemies burnt down,
And stripped off their power.
He remained the one,
The only superpower.
There wasn't war,
The ocean at peace,
There wasn't bloodshed,

His life was at ease.

Years passed by,

No one to defeat him,

Not one of them dared,

To stand against him.

'The Sole Emperor' he thought,

But in a 'land of fools'

a voice he heard.

'The Sole Emperor' he reassured,

'but in a land of fools' the voice,

It reassured.

All these years, he had no one to win,

All these years, he had no defeat,

For sole power did he commit the sin,

But now he craved for somebody to compete.

His wish remained a wish,

Until he died,

Friends as to Support is to

Enemies as to Growth. He whispered

Losing the battle,

Only he fought.

Like a Rolling Stone

Love & Loss

The Final Hour

I've started to forget; the way I loved you.

On a warm summer noon, and a canopy sky blue.

I thought it was forever, you, my lover,

But little did i know, it was the final hour.

Shall we start o'er again;

Or should i just numb my pain.

Trace your path back cause I'm turning insane.

Can we get back once again?

I ain't freezing on a summer day,

I'm sure you know i am okay.

I ain't waiting for your warm breath-

To warm me down again, I bet.

I've started to forget, the way you held my arms tight,

Along the ancient empty streets on a moon-lit cloudy
night.

I thought it was forever, you, my lover,

But little did i know. It was the final hour.

Won't you call me. One day. At my wakeup hour?

I just hope you are happy, wherever you are.

I wish i could live in oblivion

But you won't know. How I'm feeling.

You didn't give me back my heart,

I felt the same for you from the start

Why did you take my smile with you?

Leaving painful memories, not a few.

I've started to forget; the way you smile,

The one. That made me love you for a while

I thought I'd see em forever, you, my lover,

But little did I know. It was the final hour.

The Chords Incomplete

The melancholy in the air spreads around
This is an emotion familiar yet newfound.
The new fragrance in the air as it spreads
Yet the melancholy stays, the fragrance has fled.

A chaotic mind blabbers aimlessly
A Frantic heart beats tirelessly
Like the rhythm of a drop of water,
On an early winter quarter.

I just couldn't rest or resist but wander
Somewhere unknown in search of you and ponder.
Like a weary and homeless traveler against the time
Looking for a home in you, a ringing chime.

Unveiling

Thousands of hearts, yet one story to tell;
Rising above when you cast that spell;
Stirring my mind, making stories untold
Whispering them, as good as gold.
Looking at the world with an all-new feeling
Never knew what was next, unveiling
The smile i clicked, the pixels unfaded
Screaming in silence, the moment i waited.
Your voice in my ears, echoing my name.
Blazing heart roaring, living by the flame.
Slowly you noticed my mind did explode;
You knew i wanted a tad little more.

cold dreamy night, frozen on the stair
the winter breeze, against my hair.
stirring my mind, making stories untold.
whispering them, as good as gold.
words that are flowing like the wind that night
i was flying, farther away, out of sight.
leaning against the wall, i ceased to exist.
falling more into the blind mist.

your voice in my ears, echoing my name
my blazing heart roaring, i live by the flame.
i didn't just stutter when i asked for your hand
falling in love, from a faraway land.

Eyes that Smile

I open my eyes, to find you next to me.

Pulling you closer, kissing on your head.

The moment you looked at me instead

The eyes smiled, words remain unsaid.

Your fragrance on my shirt, do I yearn for;

On a dark rainy eve, when the love for you soar.

I wish you were here, to keep my heart warm-

Curl up beneath the blanket of our breath, so calm.

The strands of your hair lay on my shirt and

The eternal scars from your lips on my hand,

The one woman, I share my dreams with.

But the smile that drags me in, is still a myth.

Sliding into my arms, sinking on my chest

Baby, I don't know what to say, about the rest.

Your Voice- like I've always known, echoes in my ears.

The skin that turns me on, stranding my fears.

I knew I loved you and we ain't drifting away

I missed you every day, but you're here today.

I stood speechless, you took my breath away

Away in the dark, a beam of hope paving its way.

Your fragrance on my shirt, I did yearn for
Now that you're near, I'd yearn for more.
My heart swirling down, like a sinking ship
Down your heart into your soul, a magical trip.
On that eve, your head on my shoulders,
Couldn't ask for anything, but uphold her.
She repaired my broken heart, once again.
I held her closer to my face, and we turn insane.
I open my eyes, to find you next to me.
Pulling you closer, kissing on your head.
The moment you looked at me instead
The eyes smiled, words remain unsaid.

When Cacophony echoed Symphony

The days when we step into the darkness of the nights,

With your head resting on my lap,

and your fingers playing with my fine hair

when we expect nothing from each other but

just stay with me forever and ever.

Dreaming the wonderful days to come

Walking miles with our fingers entangled.

Our feet immersed in the wet coastal sand

Our eyes locked and we

Walk forever, until the end.

A day not far,

witnessing the light at the end of the tunnel

A pounding heart and my eyes searching

In the crowd of men and women, lurching.

When I lay my eyes on you for the first time.

My Love, Did I fall for you again, the world, sublime.

I didn't hear the great symphonies being played,

Nor did I dream of our life together, as the wind swayed.

I just closed my eyes, the moment I met you.

The moment, even cacophony echoed symphony.

The moment. I knew we were forever.

Questions Unquestioned

Why would you love me, a man drenched in misery?

Was it the nature or me, or unintended sorcery?

Was it the story of my life or my cracks in my voice.

Or the blurred dreams I had, or the depth of my choice.

Was it my pain that catapulted from my past?

Or the tiny bursts of optimism, that don't last.

Was it the way I walk, across that empty deserted station,

Or was it the smile in my eyes, that captured your attention?

Why would you love me, a man drenched in misery?

Won't you tell me why, or will it remain a mystery?

Was it the kid in me that forever thrive?

Or the man in me that never fails to strive.

Or your passion to be loved, born out of a drive.

Or did the world show you, to make me alive?

Was it the warmth and comfort, that I promise?

Or was it nature that paved it, on us?

Why would you love me, a man drenched in misery?

Won't you tell me why, or will it remain a mystery?

Thousand Miles Away

By then we had been the same person, fused in together.

A thousand miles away, but I still knew how she felt.

We had a hundred dreams that were unstoppable.

We had to work our way towards success,

maybe hard and unpredictable.

We took different paths, with our souls united.

But we promised to be together on the other side.

Until I whisper your name again, and emotions that I won't hide.

He wrote in his journal, on the first day of a tedious long-distance relationship.

Deep inside, they knew, they could work this out. Months passed without seeing her,

and many months left until he would lay his eyes on her, again.

The Video calls on a starry night

and admires her face through the phone when she sleeps.

Having second thoughts before disconnecting the call, just to adore her-

The eyes shut, and the cheeks pressed against the pillow.

He had never seen anything more innocent than that.

Through the tiny window, we lived a life, I'll never ask for again-

The urge to feel one strand of your hair on my face made me insane,

As the days and months passed by, it felt like forever.

I could see you all day, I could hear your voice, sweet as ever.

But your fragrance and the touch did I miss,

I could stretch my arms towards you, in an attempt to kiss.

But you were farther than I thought, deep within a diamond sky.

I couldn't hold you and caress you, but wait and not cry.

Those Silent Screams

A bizarre hollowness that I'd never expect to exist.

A shallow void, that could be filled. but I still can't resist.

Breaking down like an avalanche in the poles, never discovered,

My molten heart-melting me as a whole, never to recover.

I couldn't help but stand motionless, as I saw her walk farther.

I couldn't move, frozen beneath the grey skies,

I couldn't move any further.

The raindrops that fade my latent pain and-

my silhouette drenched with joy masking my tears but in vain.

An unpredictable war of the minds and the desire-

I could have won, folly or fire.

But I still couldn't take a step, was it the fear?

Or was it me sensing that the end of something beautiful was near?

A blunt needle that pierces deep into my heart,

Piercing right through, like a sharpened dart.

A pedestal over which you stood is now shattered-

I smile, when I think about the times I loved you but was disheartened.

The ruins remain blurring my vision and fogging my mind,

But I exist between the ruins, weakened, but still kind.

A Silent Lament

I'm not the man who commands, I wish to be nice

like an ancient artifact, all broken but has its price.

I'm not perfect man, you've always craved for,

But a man with flaws and passion all the more.

Not the broken man you see wandering on the streets

Not the nightmare that you see when you sleep.

I held my broken heart intact for you once again,

Please don't give up on me

The stutter when I speak, or the winks or my treat.

Or the fact that I still am not strong on my feet.

I'm not the perfect man, you've always craved for,

But a man willing to love you all the more.

But, I still stand beneath the glistening diamond stars

Healing all the thoughtful, priceless scars.

I held my broken heart intact for you once again,

Please don't give up on me.

I may be weak inside out, unlike you've ever wished.

I may not be the other men; you might think you've missed.

But I hold myself against the world, and show you, my love,

Not to be the man you've wanted, but be what you deserve.

I disappeared once and for all in the color of your eyes,
A smokescreen rather not appear of all your lies.
I held my broken heart intact for you once again,
Please don't give up on me.

One Day

The streets were empty with dry yellow leaves in the corners,

Even the barricades aligned neatly in the middle of the roads-

couldn't stop nor control my racing heartbeat, not even for a second.

My eyes shrank as they searched eagerly, my jaws felt numb.

Far away, I saw you for the first time. I smiled wholeheartedly.

I smiled uncontrollably. I was borderline hypnotized.

You were as cute as a never-ending row of red cherry blossoms.

I ran, speeding up in every step towards you.

We made memories when we were over a thousand kilometers apart.

We made memories when we were just few hundred kilometers apart.

I'd hold onto you tight, I'd wish for your fragrance to stick onto me-

Forever, never to fade away.

Your hazel brown eyes held me captivated and mesmerized.

And baby, the slight red lips had me on cuffs already.

The hair flowing hair, neatly combed, brushed against my face.

The soft cheeks pressed tight against mine.

Your arms holding me tight and mine holding yours.

How I wish to relive the moments of our first kiss-

At that moment I disappeared to places unknown.

I felt weightless, with a heavy yet content heart.

Those goodbyes every week, controlling the tears within-

Those goodbyes every week, I'd just wish that the days wouldn't end.

The streets were empty with dry yellow leaves in the corners,

Even the barricades aligned neatly in the middle of the roads-

Couldn't stop nor control my racing heartbeat, not even for a second

Every single time I meet you, I fall in love again.

The innocence in your face, and the mischiefs that you do.

Every single time I meet you, I fall in love again.

For you are, mysteriously beautiful inside out.

Unloved, Right Here

The mistakes must've been sweet but the outcomes may
not be.

One tiny mishap disrupts your pattern, never to recover,
maybe.

The whole world opens up its wondrous creations
before us.

Mesmerizing and hypnotizing us, mystic people among us.

We search for love all around this majestic sphere,

But forget that you're unloved, right here.

It wasn't a game of chess; I needn't have to think much.

No secrets or mysteries to unravel, nothing as such.

But before I could shower anyone with all the love that's
left,

Remember, you robbed the love you had for yourself,
that mighty theft.

But before you could pledge your trust to someone
else, again.

Remember to give yourself some, forgetting all the pain.

You rode down the valley, across those never-ending
range of mountains.

Where the clouds flood the grasslands, the white swans,
and the fountains.

You scream, hoping for love, to the endless dark ranges on the hillside.

They scream back, not once, but many times, yet you remain dissatisfied

For once, show some love for the person you are.

For there is no ideal man, there's none without a scar.

The pasts must have pushed you deep down underneath,

You must've gasped for breath, must've been sucked beneath.

Perfection is a myth, you aren't alone in this journey, afar-

Millions and millions raise their hands, the doors to minds ajar.

You search for love all around this majestic sphere,

But forget that you're unloved, right here.

Silence, Time & Love

Snuggled in a cozy armchair,

on a frosty balcony on a cold winter night.

So cold that our warm breath turned cold in seconds, and

her ears and slender fingers were frozen beyond
sensation.

Yet, we chose to sit, holding each other tight.

My cold fingers tucked her long black hair,
behind her ears.

We were frozen on the outside beyond sensation,

yet blanketed by our warmth, soul, and satisfaction.

The steam from the kettle filled with boiling
hot lemon tea

did a good job of giving us that subtle warmth.

The dim and flickering lights from the windows of
the other apartments,

the sounds of cars rushing past empty roads,
silence in the world,

and the soft sounds of our kisses were the only
thing the world

was awake to.

We didn't speak a word all this while,

I kissed her forehead every now and then,

and rubbed her palms to keep her warm.

She would then, place her palms on my cheeks and ears to keep me warm. Yet, we didn't speak a word all this while, but the

silence had incredible meaning, a meaning beyond the comprehension of a commoner. The time wasn't slow. nor was it

fast. The time paused itself to look and admire a magnificent

unraveling of a slow love in a fast generation.

It all Ended, Unfortunately

I wake up teary-eyed, the reasons remain unknown,
Drenched in inexplicable distress than you've ever known
I learned to live life for you, falling in love slowly,
But it all ended, unfortunately.
I craved your complete attention every single day,
Engraving the way that you smile, and love you in every way.
Remember your fragrance and dancing alone in a room not far away-
Wishing I could hold your arms and waist tight, as we sway.
But I woke up teary-eyed, wishing you'd stay longer -
Drenched in more dilemma and disbelief, oh my stranger.
*cause, I learned to live my life for you, falling in love slowly,
But it all ended, unfortunately.
I worked hard to pave my way to you through the mountains so huge,
Carrying stones and rocks so heavy, to get to you, my only refuge.
I found you between the flowing fountains in a flower garden so beautiful-

All the efforts were in vain when you decided to break
my soul.

Again, I don't leave, I don't flee and I realize.

That my heart beats for you, won't you recognize.

So, I wake up with teary eyes, in pursuit of you, I'd never
have.

Drenched in pain and sorrow, drowning so bad to never
love.

I learned to live life for you, falling in love slowly,

But it all ended, unfortunately.

The fear in my Heart

There was a time when I was naïve and lonely.
When love was an island so far away,
The times when I didn't believe that-
I could love someone, but then I saw you.
But there's a fear in my heart,
Won't you be mine from the start?
I sat all alone, wishing you were here with me.
I sat all alone, holding you so closely.
The days when I see you walking down the streets,
Your long hair flowed as you walked toward me.
But I couldn't help but mesmerize, and hypnotize-
At the psychedelic effect on me, from your eyes.
But there's a fear in my heart,
Won't you be mine from the start?
I sat all alone, craving your warmth.
The warmth I'd wish to blanket myself forever.
The little things you do are etched in my mind-
The smile that lightens my mood, is one of a kind.
Like an explorer waiting for the treasure far away,
Sculpting the perfect path for you, and I'm on my way.
But when I open my eyes and switch to reality-
I realize you were never there; I'd fail to believe it.

But all the worlds will say, that you are mine,

Only mine, you're my pursuit, I'll pursue with time.

But there's a fear in my heart,

Won't you be mine from the start?

I sat all alone, wishing you were here with me.

I sat all alone, holding you so closely.

Beginning from the end.

Are you aware of the phrase?

Beginning from the end?

It's when you have everything figured out,

When the destination is clear but the path remains hazy

Beginning from the end, reverse engineering everything.

The mind and soul, all over again.

Rebuilding your true essence.

Rediscovering love for everything.

The moment you realize that the stain caused,

By a coffee mug on your table,

Symbolizes Zen philosophy.

As they say, only the once reckless soul,

Can identify Zen, in its truest form.

Begin again, not from the beginning,

But from the end,

Your journey is longer now,

You are already a phenomenon,

You have to trace your path back to the roots,

And then return to be a phenomenon.

The journey is vital,

The process is to be enjoyed,

The process of rebuilding and rediscovering,

Is to be revered without complain.

And one day, at dawn,

When you wake up to the sounds of the birds,

When the chilly air gushes through the open windows,

When there is meaningful silence in your soul,

And nature's melody and rhythm begins,

With the sounds of the mild rain,

And a gentle breeze, you'd see

The dim ray of sunlight through the dark clouds,

You'll understand, that you've reached your destination.

Cast Your Dancing Spell on Me

Visual Imagery

The Pub 83

This emotion wasn't very new to me, right now, I'm a struggling 25-year-old trying to make a mark in this universe. A man, who still struggles to pay his bills, who walks miles to save up cash. A man who uses every opportunity on his way to showcase his talent, while rejoicing at the glance of every paycheck, although poorly paid. The emotion I'm talking about is the feeling of numbness in the moments I believed I would be excited. It was the early 1970s when I left my home aspiring to be in the show business, Like the stars of the glorious 1970s, I wanted to be one of them. With the money I had when I started off I hired a Local photographer, Simon, and began clicking fancy pictures of me to send them off to the production houses everywhere. Marlon Brando? No! James Dean? Hell No! Robert Redford! Oh boy no! I was more of a Peter Sellers, back in school, they call me the Funny Man'. I loved making jokes, there was something great about it. But, I dreamt bigger, I wanted to make the whole world laugh at my jokes and shenanigans

'Hey you!", I heard a voice, as I was immersed in a chain of thoughts. I looked around. "Hey!", the voice echoed down the hallway of the local pub 83, this time there was a tinge of agitation in the voice. "Better be on stage." The voice echoed again, I knew it was for me. I rushed down the hallway with a heavy heart, I've never liked being treated like that.

Drenched in agony, I got on stage, truck drivers from different parts of the state assembled there holding huge glasses of beer pouring down the edges, the giggles, the slurs, the burps and the quarrels made the place look like a tornado-stuck hen house. My eyes welled up, as I watched at the unwilling crowd. My eyes turned red with agony, yet I began- "Evening Gentlemen!" My voice cracked as I stuttered while telling my first line that evening.

My lips trembling looking at the crazy crowd busy in their own world.

"And that's a CUT", the director screamed through the microphone.

"Fine performance kid!" He added, as he patted on my back, gently and moved forward adjusting his funky director's hat.

I've become an actor, finally, the guy I played in this movie felt like me. I was happy to be a recognized character actor in this legendary industry.

The TV shuts down, as I wore my oversized shirt and trousers, and looking at myself in the mirror a hundred times before leaving to the pub in my street. The Pub 83.

The Noise

The smoke from the ash tray, and the dropped cigarette butts filled the right side of the table, crumbled papers lay on the floor, and a precious type writer lay still, untouched, weaving a folklore. The Aging writer, the author of an award winning novel sat in front of the typewriter for hours, smoking up cigarettes over cigarettes, clouding his mind with the smokes, blinding his vision in search of inspiration.

"Crime drama with a romantic sub plot." He murmured in his deep baritone voice. The greying stubble and receding hairline, and the horn rimmed spectacles that slide down to the end of his nose, made him look like a writer all the more.

"No No!" He said. "A pure tragic romance." He added, lifting his arms in the air, The right hand holding the cigarette carefully. He was envisioning now the story would flow. He was envisioning how his work would be different from the ones produced by the previous writers. His mind jumping from one thought to another, he dropped his arms onto the dusty table with a thud.

"The best-selling author of 1967." He murmured, the cigarette shifting from one corner of his mouth to the next, "in ruins now." He added hastily, he looked restless, the wrinkles on his forehead had stories to tell, stories of poverty, homelessness and the career in ruins.

The newspapers and the dailies called him the-"One time wonder" in the dawn of 1970s, back when he was young and handsome, when his beautiful physique and well-groomed hair won him the attention of many women, many of whom were his readers. As time passed, all his associations and collaborations failed, proving the statements made by the news true, proving it so deep that the writer himself lost the belief in himself.

"One time wonder." The writer smiled as he typed the statement on his typewriter outrageously. He sat back, on his arm chair, looking out of the window, as he has done for 30 long years, searching for inspirations, clouding his mind, bathed in smoke, breathing smoke, waiting for him. his abilities that he refrained from believing in, his words that he couldn't put down, his passion that he drowned in the voice of other people's opinions. To vanish like a smoke into pure nothingness.

On the Other Side

Gazing at the city, the towering sky scrapers, the zooming cars with the fanciest designs, the technological golden age when everything happens with the click, or a swipe or by just uttering a wish to the device, as if it were a genie and a whole generation that forgot how it is to look at each others faces on the street and exchanging smiles.

The world has become faster, and life reached the dead end for a average person and the teens wish to become billionaires and whiz kids and wunderkinds before they become adults. There was no rain on the other side of the river, the hustle and bustle of a business centre was evident as the chaos within the chaotic minds of the people remained prevalent. The sky didn't look like one, instead it was a filled with a underwhelming shades of grey beautified by the filters and apps in the phone. The receding hair line of a 19 year old commuting to his university, the wrinkles and dark circles sucking the youth out of the youth. I watch them all, helplessly in pain.

Helpless, unable to comprehend the plight, the reason for the hustle, the reason for this never ending bustle.

I stand up, holding onto my cane, my eyes still gazing at the other side of the river. 'One day when they're old, they'd miss everything they could have done as a youngster.' I thought to myself, before retiring back to my house standing steady from the gos, I have a roof over my head and the will to love forever. The man retires.

Smoke Rings of My Mind

Midnight Musings

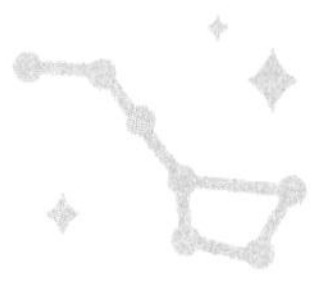

The subtle love in the eyes,
The content and the smile,
The comfort of the hug,
As if your whole world is
Caressing you.
The moment I realize,
Only you care for me,
Following the great ones
that brought me
Into this dreadful land.
The moment I realize,
This is what love is,
Love ain't a stunt,
It ain't an eruption within,
It ain't a sand castle,
Washed away by the raging tides,
But a fort standing strong,
Invincible, growing stronger with time.

I dreamt of the magnificent,
The revolutionary machines,
The future of the world,
The magnificent structure,
The magnanimity & pride,
And my mind behind it all.
But nothing works,
I lay on my back,
Scrolling through
another man's dream,
And laying envious.

Often times I wonder,

Life gives you the freedom to choose between

You being the undefeated Protagonist

or the diabolical antagonist,

Of your own story.

We decide to choose neither.

And that moment,

When we run away from making a decision,

When you realize you are indecisive,

When you realize you are incapable,

Of success, learning and everything that follows

You are already a devastating antagonist!

Often times, you think the best for others,
You hope the best for them, wholeheartedly,
Yet wish the worst for yourself,
Subconsciously.
The string of never ending self-taunts,
And the never ending rants that follow,
A vicious cycle, I don't wish for anyone.
An epiphany that striked
in the middle of the night,
When I'm made to create,
To make mistakes, to fall and rise,
Just to fall again,
And rise back stronger
Until you know my name!

I smiled as I tossed the file onto the tea table near the arm chair in the living room. I was lost in thought, a stream of emotions, nostalgia and weird emotion of remorse filled me up. The opportunities that I pushed away, the way I did with people around me. When I embraced solitude because the world around me was getting too complicated to comprehend, and when I was affected by solitude. The time that I wasted, and the choices that I made. The blessings that were bestowed upon me, and my two-year journey-

The lights were dim and the path was dark,

Yet I chose to move forward, the same old path.

The path was bad, holes and thorns,

Yet I wanted to walk on them forever,

Where did it take me to?

I had no clue.

But I knew the destinations derived-

From a path like this would be beautiful.

Hence, I kept walking for days,

Across places, and new people-

My journey along the,

Ancient Empty Streets.